# 50 Ways to Discipline Your Toddler

**Jessica Riley**

50 Ways to Discipline Your Toddler.

ISBN-13: 978-1948040020
ISBN-10: 1948040026

First Edition: November 2017
10 9 8 7 6 5 4 3 2 1

# CONTENTS

CONTENTS ................................................................. 3

INTRODUCTION ............................................................. 6

CHAPTER 1: HEALTHY EATING HABITS ....................................... 11

    1. FOOD IS YOUR BODY'S FUEL ......................................... 16

    2. PETER PIPER PICKED A PECK OF PICKLED PEPPERS ..................... 17

    3. SMOOTH MOVE SMOOTHIES! .......................................... 18

    4. WE ARE WHAT WE EAT .............................................. 19

    5. DINNER FOR DESSERT .............................................. 20

CHAPTER 2: SOCIAL SETTINGS ............................................. 21

    6. DISENGAGING VAPOR-LOCK .......................................... 24

    7. THE EXCITEMENT OF NEW THINGS .................................... 25

    8. THE SCAVENGER HUNT .............................................. 26

    9. LET'S CALM DOWN ................................................. 27

    10. "SAY, CHEESE!" ................................................. 28

CHAPTER 3: TIME MANAGEMENT ............................................. 29

    11. THE SCHEDULE ................................................... 31

    12. ROCKIN' AROUND THE CLOCK ....................................... 32

    13. LOWER YOUR EXPECTATIONS ........................................ 33

14. ISO: LITTLE HELPER ............................................................. 35

15. MINI-BREAKS ..................................................................... 36

**CHAPTER 4: SIBLINGS: "LET'S GET READY TO RUMBLE!"** ................. 37

16. THE PLAIN WHITE T'S—THE T-SHIRT ...................................... 40

17. THE LIVING ROOM STAGE ROLE-PLAYING. ............................... 41

18. COMPROMISE ..................................................................... 42

19. VALIDATE .......................................................................... 43

20. "WHAT DO YOU THINK?" ...................................................... 44

**CHAPTER 5: PARENT BEHAVIOR** .............................................. 45

21. GIVING BACK ..................................................................... 47

22. DATE DAY ......................................................................... 48

23. THE TODDLER WHISPERER .................................................... 49

24. CAREGIVER CONSISTENCY .................................................... 50

25. R-E-S-P-E-C-T .................................................................... 51

**CHAPTER 6: ENCOURAGING POSITIVE BEHAVIOR** ...................... 52

26. PICASSO ........................................................................... 55

27. NO LOSERS ........................................................................ 56

28. EMOTIONS CHART ............................................................... 57

29. THINKING CORNER .............................................................. 58

30. SELF-CONTROL ................................................................... 59

**CHAPTER 7: I SAID "NO!" & MEANING IT** .................................. 60

31. GERMS ............................................................................. 63

32. TREAT ALL THINGS, BIG & SMALL, WITH TLC ............................ 64

33. PLAY NICELY ...................................................................... 65

34. ACT SILLY .......................................................................... 66

35. BREATHE. REMAIN CALM ...................................................... 67

**CHAPTER 8: THE BORED CHILD** ............................................... 68

36. THE GREAT IPHONE DEBATE .................................................. 70

37. Simple Times Toys ............................................... 71

38. Set It Aside ..................................................... 72

39. Too Many Toys! ............................... ................. 73

40. Toddler Gone Wild ............................................. 74

**CHAPTER 9: NIGHTY NIGHT ......................................75**

41. The Silent Treatment............................ ............ 78

42. Transition Time ................................................. 79

43. Say No To Techno! ............................................. 80

44. Excuses To Get Up .......................................... 81

45. The Boogeyman ......................................... ....... 83

46. Essential Oils ................................................... 84

47. White Noise ..................................................... 85

48. Bore Them To Sleep ............................... ........ 86

49. Guardian of the Bedroom Galaxy ....................... 87

50. Love Always and Forever ................................. 88

**CONCLUSION ...................................................89**

**FINAL WORDS ..................................................94**

# Introduction

*"Toddler (noun): Emotionally unstable pint-sized dictator with the uncanny ability to know exactly how far to push you towards utter insanity before reverting to a loveable creature." -Unknown*

Does it seem like you are spending your days following your toddler from room to room, cleaning up their path of destruction?

Do you feel like you've done everything within your power to keep them from destroying everything and anything that's within their reach?

Have you dreamed of booking a one-way ticket to Fiji?

Ever have the desire to hide under the mountain of

laundry that's waiting to be folded and put away?

Did you find yourself nodding your head to any or perhaps even all of the above? If so, please understand that you are not alone. I definitely hear you. I've pretended to book more flights on Travelocity.com than I can count on two hands!

This parenting thing ain't easy! You've heard this before—parenting is the most challenging, stressful job there is, harder than any other job out there.

But, it also comes with the most rewards. The unconditional love you feel for and receive from your child is something only a parent can experience, and that's a beautiful privilege that we sometimes can take for granted.

Graduating from being the parent of a newborn to the parent of a toddler is a big and monumental step.

During the newborn phase, you are basically in survival mode. You feel the weight of the world on your shoulders as you try your best to raise another human being—that didn't come with an instruction manual. And, if it's your first born, you are probably in a permanent state of sleep deprivation, as well as suffering from constant worry that you are going to do something that will cause catastrophic, irreversible damage to your bundle of joy. Damage so severe it will affect them forever and probably even prevent them from making it into their first choice Ivy League college.

Now, as the parent of a toddler, it's a totally different ballgame. You are laying critical groundwork and the foundation to be built upon for the rest of their lives.

If there are any gaps or cracks in the foundation, what happens when the house is built? It might crumble and falling apart beneath their little feet!

No pressure, right? Well, thankfully you are a great parent who only wants to do what's best for your child.

How could I possibly know that? You picked up this book of your own free will, right? Nobody forced you to do it? Well then, that's how I know you're a great parent. You are actively seeking out support in overcoming an obstacle—Toddler Discipline 101.

If you weren't looking for help in bettering your situation, you'd just keep doing the same thing over and over again, expecting and praying for different results each time. That's a popular definition of the word insanity, and unfortunately is an approach all too often applied by frustrated, albeit hopeful, parents!

As a mom of four kids, I've learned a great deal from reading parenting books and attending childhood behavior conferences, but I've learned most of what I know from my own personal experience. I actually had four kids ages four and under at one point—now *that's* the definition of insanity!

There is so much information and advice out there on toddler discipline, it can actually be overwhelming. There are tons of parenting books, Pinterest boards and mommy blogs with tons of information. Being a busy parent—who has time to track down and weed through all that advice?

Great news, you don't have to! I've done the work for you. I was overwhelmed too, when I was trying to deal with *my* toddlers.

That's why I wrote this book, based on my own experience, as well tips from stacks and stacks of books I read about discipline for my own toddlers during those crazy years.

I put together all my advice, insight and tips, then chose my top 50, resulting in this book I call, *50 Ways to Discipline Your Toddler*, covering all the important topics, including:

healthy eating habits, social settings, siblings, parent behavior, and so much more.

After reading this book, you will have a clear idea what to do to have a happy, well behaved toddler.

Whenever you're ready, turn to the next page, and let the fun begin...

# Chapter 1: Healthy Eating Habits

Many psychologists specializing in child behavior would agree that one of the most critical components of figuring out the root cause of a behavioral issue would be nutrition. Before assessing or looking into anything else that might be playing a factor in a child's behavior—an assessment of their diet is super important.

Is the child getting all the essential vitamins and nutrients they need to support proper growth and development? Are they getting enough nutrients from the various food groups? Are the children partaking in any kind of dietary restriction that could cause them to be more susceptible to a specific nutrient deficiency? How are they making up for that nutrient deficiency?

In our household my husband and I were eating a vegetarian diet—until our son started showing signs of anemia, that is. He was tired, not normally considered bad when you're talking about a nearly 2 year old, but he was *super* tired—sleeping 18-20 hours a day. His blood panel came back showing he was very low on iron. So, lean meat was immediately introduced back into the family diet. After only a couple months, his iron was well within the normal-range.

A healthy, well-rounded diet is vital for brain and physical development.

The human body doesn't perform as well on cognitive or physiological tests when it's lacking in key nutrients. Your child should eat a wide array of colorful fruits and vegetables, protein, healthy fats, and grains. Processed foods and sugar should be very limited.

## The 3 Most Common Nutrient Deficiencies in Children:

**Protein**: Important for maintaining a healthy immune system. It's also vital in muscle and tissue growth and repair.

> *Excellent Protein Sources:* Lean meat, peanut butter (preferably all-natural and very low in sugar), eggs, cheese, tofu, Greek yogurt, and beans.

**Iron**: Necessary to create healthy red blood cells that deliver oxygen around the body and brain.

> *Excellent Iron Sources:* Leafy green vegetables, tempeh, quinoa, dried peaches and apricots, spirulina.

**Vitamin D**: Essential for bone health and it also plays an important part in supporting the immune system and protecting against depression.

> *Excellent Vitamin D Sources:* Salmon, egg yolks, cottage cheese, and fish.

Other causes for many toddler meltdowns can be low blood sugar and/or dehydration. They might not be officially diagnosed as having hypoglycemia, but after a long day at daycare or at Grandma's house, they really could have low blood sugar. Low blood sugar causes irritability, headaches, fatigue, confusion, and anger. If they are running around a lot and perspiring without replenishing with fluids, they could also become dehydrated.

When an adult has low blood sugar or is dehydrated, they feel the hunger pangs or thirst and recognize it as, 'I'm hungry, I better go eat something,' or 'I'm feeling a little dizzy, I really need some water.' A child doesn't recognize these symptoms as such and just feels more and more irritable and angry. It's up to the adults to recognize the signs that the child is hungry or needs water.

Thankfully, as soon as your child eats or drinks something, typically within a matter of minutes they should feel wonderful and be back to their happy little self once again.

# 1. Food Is Your Body's Fuel

Make sure you child is getting proper nutrition. You can do this by starting a daily food journal and then either doing your own research to find any nutritional gaps, or you could make an appointment with your pediatrician to go over your child's daily food intake.

An example: If your child has low iron and is borderline anemic, you might be seeing symptoms like irritability, fatigue, and lack of focus or inability to concentrate. The night and day difference you will see when a nutritional deficit is corrected can be quite amazing. Once the gap is filled, parents have seen noticeable results in a matter of a few days.

# 2. Peter Piper Picked a Peck of Pickled Peppers

If you are struggling to get your picky toddler to eat vegetables and/or fruit, allow them to help you pick out produce at the farmer's market or grocery store.

When toddlers are actively participating in the process, like doing an incredible job at picking out the perfect red peppers, they feel a sense of accomplishment and are more likely to eat something they got to help out with.

# 3. Smooth Move Smoothies!

Smoothies are a great way to give your child the proper nutrition they need without having to deal with any tantrums from the child, or tears of frustration (from you).

It doesn't have to be exact science. Something simple like tossing a handful of spinach, a cup of vanilla Greek yogurt, a few berries, almond milk, and ice cubes in a blender will provide an excellent source of iron, vitamin D, and protein.

Get creative and have some fun with this!

# 4. We Are What We Eat

Story time and role playing.

Read a book about farm animals and then discuss what the animals eat. Then, turn that into a discussion on what people eat and why it's so important for us to eat nutritious food.

## 5.      Dinner For Dessert

Many parents have their child sit at the table until they eat what is on their plate. This can work, but it often involves a lot of tears and angry outbursts.

An alternative to this would be to allow the child to get up and go, but save their plate of food. When your child comes to you later to ask for something to eat, present them with their plate of food. Do not give them anything else until they have finished what's on their plate.

# Chapter 2: Social Settings

If you are having a challenging time disciplining your toddler at home, it's probably an absolute nightmare when you are out in public, especially when confronted with a temper tantrum.

I remember being in the dairy aisle at the grocery store when one of the twins, who were two at the time, opened a cooler and pulled out a yogurt. Before I had a chance to react, she had thrown it onto the floor, spilling yogurt everywhere. My eyes welled up with tears of embarrassment. For a split second I thought that any minute now her head was going to spin around in circles. Exorcism in Aisle 3, anyone?

Do you ignore the behavior and let them 'get it all out,' or bribe them to behave with treats or new toys? Or, stop, drop, and run—leaving everything you were doing behind to get to the car as fast as humanly possible? No! All no! These are all the wrong ways to handle an outburst or meltdown in a public setting or social situation.

I'm going to let you in on some secrets. Here is my best advice, and tips I've used with all four of my kids that got through many a child's outburst in a public setting. After reading some of these words of wisdom, hopefully you'll be able to tackle any social event or shopping excursion with confidence and maybe even, dare we say, excitement.

Okay, maybe not that far, but you get the picture.

# 6. Disengaging Vapor-Lock

If your toddler starts screaming and crying due to being overtired or hungry, it's extremely tough to get them out of this 'vapor-lock,' but you can do it! Find a quiet part of the store or wherever you may be. While they are busy screaming and whimpering, start whispering to them. Start with soothing words and repeat them. Be almost inaudible. Don't try to rationalize with them or bribe them, just speak soothing words over and over again until they start to quiet down and look at you. They will get quiet and try to hear what you're saying. It's now that you can get through to them and be heard.

Getting a child out of vapor-lock is a must if you want to get any dialogue going with them. If you are trying to talk or yell at a child that's in vapor-lock mode, you are better off trying to talk to the wall. Counter-acting their hyperemotional, irrational, loud state by being just the opposite should help you immensely in getting them to calm down, buying you time to finish up what you are doing.

# 7. The Excitement of New Things

Have special toys and books only for outings. You can keep them in your purse or in a separate bag to be used only on outings. Do not let them play with these special things at home, or you will completely defeat the purpose.

The excitement of a new toy or book can't be matched. The things they are already familiar with and love won't achieve the excitement and full attention of something that is new.

# 8. The Scavenger Hunt

Make it a game!

Kids love adventures. Show some pictures of things you really need to find and enlist their help in finding them! Make it a big deal when they do find what they're looking for.

This game gives them something to focus on instead of what they were initially upset about. The fine art of distraction.

# 9.    Let's Calm Down

If you are at a store and have a cart or basket full of items and must get out of the store, find a store worker, and ask them to put your items aside for you. Go out to the car and have a bit of 'calm down' session. Play some of their favorite music. Are they hungry? Dig a granola bar from your purse. Just calm them down. Explain to them that you need to go back into the store to finish up the shopping and it would be of great help if they could help you by being on their best behavior.

It might even help if you told them the things on your list. "First, we'll go and get bananas, then we'll grab some lettuce, and then... we are all done!" Kids are great at processing lists and tasks.

# 10. "Say, Cheese!"

If you're shopping and nothing seems to be working to quiet them down, pull out the nearly fool-proof method—the cellphone.

What child isn't enamored with a cellphone or electronic device? Set your phone on airplane mode to prevent them from making calls or hopping onto your Facebook app. Make sure they can securely hold it. Allow them to be the 'movie maker.' If they don't already know how to snap pictures, give them instructions on how to do so. Tell them to document your 'adventure'!

Warning: be prepared to delete a 'few' pictures.

# Chapter 3: Time Management

Routine. Routine. Routine. This can't be emphasized enough! Toddlers do best if they have a consistent routine to follow. They need the predictability that comes with having a reliable schedule. It's important to set a schedule for naps, playtime, meals, and snacks.

When your child knows ahead of time what's coming next, they will be less likely to take a turn for tantrum-ville. The transition will be much easier than just going from playtime at the park to nap time when the day before you did playtime at the park, then lunch or story time.

"But I don't have a set schedule and my child is 2½, is it too late?" Not at all! You can start setting a schedule immediately. The crucial thing to remember though is consistency. It's not going to have instantaneous results and you might get discouraged, but you must stay consistent. A reliable routine will definitely pay off. It might take a week or maybe even a couple of months, but it will yield positive results.

# 11. The Schedule

Setting a schedule is important for any child, but especially for a toddler.

They need to know what to expect, what's coming next in their day. It helps their developing brains prepare and process, which eliminates the meltdowns that occur from being confused, overwhelmed or disappointed.

Think of what it's like as an adult when your day suddenly takes a turn you weren't prepared for. Maybe you have a lunch date planned with friends, but your boss calls a last minute meeting. What are you feeling? Well, take that feeling and amplify it 100 times, that's what a toddler feels. Is it any surprise that sometimes they have temper tantrums? Especially when things are chaotic or not going as they usually do?

# 12. Rockin' Around The Clock

Teach them how to tell time and provide them with a watch. This not only allows them to learn how to tell time, it builds responsibility, and a sense of independence.

This also can teach time management skills— something they will need for the rest of their lives.

Jessica Riley

# 13. Lower Your Expectations

For the parent, time management skills are also a critical component of keeping yourself sane. You need to cut yourself some slack and get real.

Taking care of a toddler, and trying tc keep your house spotless and clutter free 24/7? Not going to happen, so don't set your expectations there.

Should you have other children, eldercare responsibilities, a job or other commitments, this applies as well, perhaps even more so. Unreasonable expectations will only cause you to be discouraged and feel disappointed in yourself. These are dangerous emotions than can quickly turn into feelings of guilt and depression. Steer clear.

Invest in a stop watch or use the clock on your kitchen stove. Set certain time limits for specific household tasks. Twenty minutes for laundry, or twenty minutes for making beds, etc. When the timer goes off, it doesn't matter where you are at in that task—you are done for the day. During those Twenty minutes you are 100% committed and focused on the task at hand. You will be surprised at how much more you can get accomplished by breaking household tasks up into twenty minute increments and

33

spreading them throughout your day.

# 14. ISO: Little Helper

Hire your little helper. Yes, it is likely going to take you more time to clean or make dinner, but it will keep your little one busy and content.

They love feeling helpful and needed. Kids, especially little ones, enjoy the time spent with you doing something that in their eyes makes them seem grown up.

# 15. Mini-Breaks

Let's say your little one is acting out while you are on the phone, working from home or just trying to get a project done. Tell them that you are going to spend fifteen minutes playing with them and then go back to work for thirty minutes. Adjust the times to whatever works for you.

Make sure you stick to your word and completely set the other work aside. Those fifteen minutes are for only your child. Act silly and crazy, have some fun! But, when those fifteen minutes are up, let your child know that you now have to return to what you were doing, but will be back in thirty minutes to have some more fun!

# Chapter 4: Siblings: "Let's Get Ready to Rumble!"

It's so much fun growing up with a sibling. There is always someone around to play with, and you have your best friend around 24/7!

Yes, that is true. But, only for about 40% of the time. The other 60% of the time is spent screaming that 'so-and-so is looking at me!' or 'so-and-so is breathing on me!' or my favorite, 'so-and-so is thinking mean about me!'

Siblings definitely have a love-hate and hate-love relationship. My youngest two are twins, so I know this sibling rivalry situation all too well.

Most, if not all, of a child's behavior towards one another is directly related to their birth order—if they are the oldest, middle, or the youngest child. Birth order determines a lot about a child's personality, and what their interactions with other children and adults will look like.

Typically, oldest children pride themselves on being more independent. They carry an air of confidence, and tend to be bossy towards younger siblings. The youngest child is more dependent on others for help and can be whiny. The middle child is stuck smack dab in the middle of two rather distinct personalities. They seem to be always looking for attention—good or bad—it doesn't seem to matter to them!

"Let's get ready to rumble!!"

Take those personalities and throw them all together in a big bowl, mix with a whisk, and you have the ingredients for one heck of a WWF wrestling match, a colossal meltdown, or both!

Here I give you some ideas and thoughts on dealing with sibling rivalry and misbehavior associated with siblings.

# 16. The Plain White T's — The t-shirt.

We have all seen the pictures floating around on social media of the kids stuck in the white t-shirt, right? Well, there's a reason for that. Not only is it hysterical to see two sullen faced kids nose-to-nose, stuck in an oversized white t-shirt, it is also an effective disciplinary method!

Have an oversized t-shirt at the ready for when your kids start name-calling or fighting. Place them both in the shirt facing each other for a designated amount of time, or until they give each other a real hug and apologize to one another. If there's more than two children involved, have them take turns.

# 17. The Living Room Stage Role-playing.

Have the children sit down and relax. Let them calm down a bit. Then, explain that you are going to do a role-playing exercise. Have each child act out (no words) what their sibling did to them, including how it made them feel. After the children have done their part, then you can discuss the issues, hopefully with a little more understanding and reason from both sides.

This is an exercise that isn't just great for kids, adults can benefit from it, too.

# 18. Compromise

A toddler is not too young to learn conflict resolution skills. This is an extremely beneficial skillset that will only serve to help them in all aspects of their lives. Demonstrate positive conflict resolution skills, such as teaching them to compromise. What does compromise mean? When you hear the start of an argument or fight brewing, jump in and show them exactly what it means to compromise.

It is important to demonstrate how to compromise and actually show them during real-life situations. After a few times, have them suggest ideas, and get them more involved in the process.

# 1 9 .  V a l i d a t e

Respect and validate the feelings that your children have. Don't just brush them under the rug, they will only re-surface at a later date. Take care of it now. No time like the present!

Let them know their feelings and emotions are important to you.

# 20. "What Do You Think?"

Ask your children for disciplinary advice. Given their behavior and actions, what do they believe the most appropriate and fair punishment should be? How can they make sure they don't repeat their offense? Will the punishment keep them from making the errors in judgement?

Let them give their answers and then you give yours. Now would be the perfect time to bring up the word 'compromise.'

# Chapter 5: Parent Behavior

*"Tell me and I forget. Teach me and I learn. Involve me and I remember." -Benjamin Franklin*

One of the most important things you can do as a parent is to establish a good, positive relationship with your child. By building that bond now, they will learn to trust you, and will come to you when they are having problems instead of keeping them bottled up inside. It isn't good to brush their concerns off or belittle them. Listen and validate their concerns. Repeat back to them what they told or confided to you—this lets them know that you heard them.

Even during the toddler years, if they come up to you, make a point to put down the phone or magazine, and give them your complete and undivided attention. Now, honestly, this can't be done 100% of the time, life happens! Don't freak out or feel guilty about it, as long as they know they are loved and are the most important priority in your life, everything will be great.

"What do you mean 'Parent Behavior?' How should parents behave? Is there something we should be doing or demonstrating as parents that can have a positive impact on your child?" Absolutely. Your kids are watching you, even when you don't think they are.

# 21. Giving Back

Don't just tell your child about compassion. Teach them and show them what compassion is. It's never too early to take them to an animal shelter to drop off a bag of dog treats, or to a nursing home to bring Christmas cards.

It's amazing how a child's behavior can shift when they learn about compassion. 'Giving back' to help others in need helps not only the children but parents too. If you are feeling super stressed out and overwhelmed with everything going on in your life, giving back to a cause will make you feel better about your situation almost instantly. And, a happy mom and/or dad is a happy child!

# 22. Date Day

Instead of bribing with toys or treats, use time spent with mom and/or dad as a reward. Take your child out on a 'date.' It could include going out for lunch, a matinee movie, the park, or whatever else they'd like to do. It's their day.

Date days are great to do at the end of the week because that can be the motivation for good behavior throughout the week. Use gentle reminders during the week that 'eating all your dinner' or 'not hitting your sister in the head with your beach ball' will earn them a date—a day that's all about them.

# 23. The Toddler Whisperer

If your child is misbehaving and talking back or yelling at you, it can be really tempting to yell back. Please don't do this! This only teaches the child that getting upset and angry and yelling go hand in hand.

You can handle it several different ways, including whispering. Instead of reacting by yelling back, lower your voice to a barely audible whisper. Don't raise your voice. Let them get curious. As they get curious as to why you are whispering, they will slowly start to come out of their vapor-lock angry state, allowing you to talk to them.

Don't stop whispering. Keep it up. See if they can whisper with you. Toddlers usually love this game and find it funny. Try and tell them why yelling isn't nice and why lowering their voice and talking about what's wrong is a lot better. Explain that when they are yelling you can't understand a word they are saying, but if they talk softly and like a big boy or girl you can understand and help them with whatever it is they are upset about.

# 24. Caregiver Consistency

It is vital that whatever behavioral correction you take with your child that it's consistent across the board. Whoever your child's primary caregivers are, they must all be on board with what behavior you will and will not tolerate, and what suitable consequences are.

If the child spends time in two different residences or attends daycare, it would also be extremely beneficial if an identical or at least similar daily schedule be followed. At the very least, abide by the same nap times.

# 25. R-E-S-P-E-C-T

Children must respect their parents and authority figures. If your child doesn't respect you, it is obvious in their behavior. They will treat what you say as optional instead of things they should or shouldn't do.

If you don't follow through with what you say you're going to do, you lose authority in the eyes of your child. If you tell them they are losing a toy because they misbehaved, but then you don't actually take it away, you have unfortunately lost some authority. Again, this hammers home the point that you must be consistent in your words and your actions. To raise good kids you must have their respect.

# Chapter 6: Encouraging Positive Behavior

*"You're off to great places! Today is your day! Your mountain is waiting...so get on your way!" -Dr. Seuss*

Have you ever had to bribe your toddler with a candy bar to keep them from throwing things out of the cart and wailing at the top of their lungs while you are standing six deep in the grocery store checkout lane with an overflowing cart? Have you been at someone else's birthday party when your tot decides they must have cake and ice cream now? Like they can't wait another minute, they need it now? I can answer yes to both. It was awful and crazy embarrassing at the time, but now looking back it's a little comical. The best part is, I survived!

If you haven't experienced either of the above situations, your day is coming. Oh boy, is it ever coming. Thankfully, you will be better prepared for how to handle this type of scenario when—not if, but when—it comes up.

I am going to show you some ways to encourage positive behavior without resorting to the good old candy bar approach. Does the candy bar approach work? Yes, it does. But, the problem is that it only works in that moment, it doesn't have a lasting effect or guide the child to appropriate behavior. Instead it reinforces your child's belief that if they throw a big enough temper tantrum or scream as loud as they possibly can, they will eventually get what they want. They must stay the course and not give up!

You need to look at some disciplinary methods that

actually serve to encourage your toddler to want to be good and reward them for doing it.

As Dr. Ross Greene, clinical psychologist and best-selling author, says, "Kids do well if they CAN." Dr. Greene believes that kids want to behave, but often times don't have the knowledge or skills to do so. They are lacking the necessary skillset to meet your expectations. What can we do to provide positive encouragement? Excellent question!

# 26. Picasso

Embrace your child's creative side. So, your toddler decides to use your living room walls as a canvas... again. You've told them countless times to stay on the paper! Crayons are for paper only!

Your normal response would be to confiscate the crayons and discipline your child. Instead, this time, praise their 'wonderful work,' and try exploring the world of art together. Show them that you are interested in art, too.

A great television program is called, *The Joy of Painting*, hosted by Bob Ross. You've more than likely seen the show or at least know who he is. He is well-known for his use of expressions like 'happy trees.' His voice is really soothing and the show is impeccably clean and perfect for all ages. Learning about art and showing how a real artist uses only paper as a canvas should flip a switch and allow coloring on walls to become a thing of the past.

# 27. No Losers

If your child is upset because they 'lost' at a game or a race, be proactive and stop the tantrum before it starts. Sit down and look them in the eye, tell them they did the very best they could, and that is what matters.

It's also important to tell them that there are no 'losers'. There are 'winners' and 'learners' and lucky them—they got to be a 'learner!' How cool is that?

# 28. Emotions Chart

Create an emotions chart. Many children have difficulty in expressing their emotions. This difficulty can rear its ugly head in displays of anger, frustration, confusion, or full blown 'four alarm fire' temper tantrums.

To help them talk through their emotions, you can create a chart. The emotions chart has a row of faces going from an angry face to a very happy face with other emotion faces in between.

It is more difficult to get your toddler to pay attention to you when they are all worked up and in the middle of a screaming fit, so bringing out the emotion chart when they are still relatively calm and capable of listening to you is best. Point to the faces and allow them to tell you which face they are. From there you can discuss why they are there and how both of you can work together to get them to the very happy face.

## 29. Thinking Corner

Have a thinking corner. Not time out, it's a thinking corner. When your toddler is all worked up and hysterical, they obviously need a time-out, but instead of a time-out, send them to the thinking corner. 'Time-out' gives them the impression they are well... 'out.' You want to change their behavior, but you don't want them to feel excluded.

Associate something positive with going to the thinking space. Make it a quiet corner or room in the house. The thinking corner can have a stack of colorful picture books and some toys like building blocks or puzzles.

# 30. Self-Control

At the toddler stage, kids are still learning self-control. If your child is prone to throwing the remote control whenever he gets his little hands on it, keep it away and out of his sight.

Being proactive and eliminating something that you know will cause undesirable behavior isn't lazy parenting, nor are you 'giving in.' What you are doing is picking your battles. A toddler should not be expected to have the ability to see the remote and then immediately think of the consequences for throwing it. He sees the remote and sees himself throwing it across the room. A five year old on the other hand should definitely be expected to have enough self-control to see the remote and not even consider throwing it. This age group may try to steal the remote and change the channel to Mickey Mouse Clubhouse instead.

# Chapter 7: I said "No!" & Meaning It

Kids that hear, 'No! No! No! No!' become immune to the word. After becoming used to it, they honestly don't really even hear it anymore. It's just another word like 'the' to their ears. It has lost all meaning.

Instead of explaining why something is bad, incorrect, or why your toddler shouldn't be doing it, you shout 'No!' Perhaps you've had a long day at work and are exhausted, or you're in the middle of fixing lunch. Whatever the reason, we all do it from time to time.

The word 'No!' is said so often to kids that the majority are desensitized to the word. Have no fear! There is hope! There are alternatives that are actually better on the ears and have shown to be more effective. It's definitely going to take some time and self-control on your part to not fall back to the old habit of saying, 'No! More than likely you were brought up hearing the word more than most—we all were.

Decide to make a conscious effort to break the habit. It's better to use phrases with a bit more explanation or reason behind them. Now, you can't dive into a huge in-depth explanation of the 'whys' and 'hows,' because at this age they wouldn't be able to comprehend or understand what you are saying. To them that would sound like nothing more than, "Blah-blah-blah, blah-blah-blah."

There are ways to remain in control as the authority figure, without use of the old standby, 'No!'

# 31. Germs

Your toddler is flipping out and causing a commotion in the middle of a clothing store. They dropped their sucker on the ground and instead of giving it back to them like they wanted, you wrapped it in paper and tossed it into the garbage.

Walk to the back of the store or to a quiet, not-too-busy department and get down to their level so you have eye contact with them. Explain that the floor is dirty and full of germs that can cause people to get sick. That you don't want him to get sick and have to stay home in bed missing out on all the fun stuff you have planned. And then there is the doctor visits that would result from being sick. Ugh. Just a mess. The sucker was thrown away to save them from potentially yucky consequences.

# 32. Treat All Things, Big & Small, With TLC

You walk into the dining room to find your toddler trying to whack the family dog in the head with a plastic bat. Instead of yelling out, 'NO!!' or screaming, use a firm but gentle tone, and tell them you are going to show them the right way to pet the doggy.

'The doggy loves it when you pet him like this,' and then demonstrate the correct way to pet the dog. Now have them try, under your supervision, to pet the dog the right way. Explain how hitting the doggy would hurt the doggy, and that's not nice, and not allowed.

# 33. Play Nicely

Your toddler has pulled his friend's hair causing her to cry. Instead of disciplining with, 'NO,' explain that pulling hair is mean and not appropriate behavior.

Let them know how to play 'gently' and 'nicely.' Would they like their hair pulled? When they answer, 'No,' ask them, 'why not?' This should help them make the connection that pulling hair equals pain.

# 34. Act Silly

Let's say you are at a store and your toddler starts picking up everything within arms-reach. Stop! I know it's tempting to shout that word, 'No!' but don't.

Immediately counter that strong impulse in you by doing the exact opposite. Start acting silly, in order to get their attention, or start playing slow-motion, chasing them outside the store.

# 35. Breathe. Remain Calm

Did you just throw your spoon at your sister? Don't say it. Don't say it!

Have them go pick it up and bring the spoon back to the table. Tell them what a spoon is used for.

If they throw it again, guess what? Repeat the process. Keep repeating the process without resorting to yelling, 'No' or showing any signs of anger or frustration in your voice.

# Chapter 8: The Bored Child

Let's get one thing out of the way. Toddlers have short attention spans, and realistically there is nothing that can be done overnight to change that. We can however improve their ability to focus and entertain themselves with their surroundings and not depend on constant stimulation and entertainment. This will improve their attention span in the long-term.

Exposure to electronic devices like iPads and tablets is occurring very early on in life. Usually, by the time a child is two years of age they have already been exposed to an iPhone or tablet. In the interest of full disclosure, my own children at the age of two, knew more about the apps on my iPhone than I did!. They learn to become entertained by dancing bears on a screen or playing a counting game by pressing a screen and watching it light up with fireworks and noise. The stimulation is intoxicating to a young child. This constant barrage of stimulation becomes something of a necessity. Sadly, they lose the ability to entertain themselves, which in turn can create behavior issues and frustrated parents.

# 36. The Great iPhone Debate

If your child plays games on your iPhone while you are waiting in the checkout line at the grocery store, or at home cooking dinner—as awful as it is to think about—it needs to stop. Handing the child an electronic device to keep them entertained may work in the short-term, but it will create major problems down the line when your 7-year old has the attention span of a toddler.

Involve your child in what you are doing, or allow them to do things that don't require technology. The game iSpy is simple and fun for all ages. It's a great game to break out in the checkout lane.

# 37. Simple Times Toys

Give your child simple activities to entertain themselves with, such as wooden blocks, alphabet letters, puzzles, or coloring books.

An overstimulated mind makes for a very moody, frustrated child.

# 38. Set It Aside

If your child is throwing a tantrum over an activity he isn't interested in playing, set the activity on the backburner. Allow them to choose the next activity or toy they would like to play with.

Explain to them that it's fine that they would like to play with one thing instead of another, but that after they are done, they must do what you would like to do. This diffuses the situation and allows the child to calm down while playing with what they want to play with.

This also is an important lesson in compromise.

# 39. Too Many Toys!

When a child is repeatedly over-stimulated and surrounded with too many toys and activities. Yes, it's true, despite what Grandma says, children CAN have too many toys. Eventually, they are going to take their toys for granted and have less appreciation for their things.

If your child starts throwing or purposefully breaking his toys, it's time for an intervention. In this situation, and taking the age of the child into consideration, it may be time to confiscate the toys.

A toddler displaying this kind of behavior needs to see the toys go with you somewhere else, out of sight. Pick up the mistreated toys and take them away.

Now, to a toddler, if they're some of his favorite toys, keeping them away for a day will seem like a lifetime. Return them, explaining why they were taken away and that you know he has learned a valuable lesson so he has earned them back. If he does it again, repeat the process.

# 40. Toddler Gone Wild

If you are trying to work or accomplish something—anything—and it's just not getting done because you have a toddler gone wild, stop what you are trying to get done. Seriously. Just stop. Now you need to figure out a way for your child to 'help' you.

Even if it's going to take you twice as long to finish folding the clothes, doing the dishes, or working on a report—it would take you more time and cause much more frustration to have to clean up any messes or be interrupted fifty hundred million times. Please, allow them to 'help.'

# Chapter 9: Nighty Night

I don't know about you, but those commercials showing parents tucking their adorable, smiling toddlers into their cozy little beds, kissing them on the cheek, saying 'Goodnight, I love you!' and then closing the bedroom door after blowing them a kiss, couldn't be FARTHER from the truth! How glorious would it be if that was indeed the case?

Myself and most of the parents I know wish they could hire someone else to come put their kids to bed. Bedtime is a battle of wills and a struggle for control. It's a test in patience.

Good news! Bedtime doesn't have to be an epic battle or struggle. It should and can turn out to be an enjoyable part of your day. Yes, enjoyable. Instead of dreading the bedtime battle, it needs to become a favorite part of your day, instead.

Due to varying naptimes and lifestyles, there is no one perfect bedtime for every toddler. But, there is one thing that is consistent across the board for toddlers that have an easier time being put to bed, and staying there—routine. Routines make bedtime much less frustrating and stressful—and some might even call it fun!

Before I get into some tips and advice on how to handle your 'strongly-willed' tot, go through this mental checklist relating to your child's bedroom environment.

• Is there a draft? Is the temperature constant and comfortable?

• Is there a nightlight? Is anything casting scary shadows on the walls?

• Does the closet door or window creak?

• Is there a comfortable bed that isn't cluttered with stuffed animals and/or other toys?

• Is there a pillow that gives proper support to the neck?

# 41. The Silent Treatment

When your toddler doesn't want to stay in bed and keeps getting up, instead of getting angry or giving up and letting him stay up with you until he falls asleep, try this. Without getting angry, but maintaining authority, being firm, guide him back to his bedroom and put him back in his bed. Each time he gets out of bed, repeat the process.

Don't talk or yell, just put him back to bed, and then leave the room. Eventually he will learn that getting out of bed doesn't do any good, because he's just going to end up back there. He will soon tire of the 'getting out of bed' game.

# 42. Transition Time

A toddler needs approximately 12-hours of sleep. If they don't get that 12-hours of sleep they are going to be sleep deprived. A sleep deprived toddler is something nobody wants. Making sure they get the full 12-hours of sleep is also crucial for important cognitive development and growth.

Having a bedtime routine is important, and being consistent with that routine is just as important. Allowing your child thirty minutes of quiet play in their room before getting tucked in for bed is a great transitionary step from a child that's had a busy day, to 'now it's time to settle down' for bed time.

Picture books are great for quiet time. A classic is Goodnight Moon by Margaret Wise Brown and Clement Hurd. It's a beautiful story with wonderfully soft, soothing-to-the-eye graphics.

# 43. Say No To Techno!

If your toddler is bouncing off the walls at bedtime, and you've eliminated sugar as the culprit, it's likely too much stimulation too close to bedtime. It's time to put a limitation on screen time. Something like no television or technology after 6:30pm.

It allows your child's brain to relax a bit and not be jumping all over the place. Instead of television, engage them in conversation, have them talk about the best parts of their day, or what they're looking forward to doing tomorrow.

You can also talk about your day and what you liked best. It makes them feel good to have you sharing a part of your day with them.

# 44. Excuses To Get Up

"One more story!!!"

"I'm thirsty!! I need a glass of water!!!"

"I'm hungry!"

These might be some of the things you hear after putting your little one to bed. It can get very, very frustrating very quickly.

When you put them to bed, you want them to stay in bed. You've most likely had a tough day and want nothing more than to curl up on the couch and either catch up with your husband, finish binge watching Game of Thrones, or just sit and enjoy total silence.

It's only human that you get irritated and angry. But, you need to stop yourself from letting that happen. If you get angry, that will just cause your child to get angry—which makes bedtime even more challenging.

Have you heard the phrase, 'Happy mom is happy baby?' Well, it's true with anger too. An angry mom is an angry baby! Keep calm, but be firm in your response to your child. It is bedtime and bedtime means they don't get to ask for any more snacks, water, etc.

# 45. The Boogeyman

Is your child afraid of the boogeyman or fearful of the dark? If so, it's super important to validate their fears and let them know that you are there for them. You would never ever let anything happen to them. They are home, and at home they will always be safe.

Don't ignore them or tell them to 'grow up.' This will only make them more fearful. If they are scared of the dark, take them to the store and allow them to choose a nightlight. Make it fun for them to pick one out. If they are scared of monsters, watch the Pixar movie Monsters, Inc., or get silly and go on a monster fighting expedition around their room—finding nothing of course.

# 46. Essential Oils

Sometimes kids have a harder time than others falling asleep. In this case, an all-natural thing you can try is aromatherapy. Essential oils like Lavender and Cedarwood are reportedly good for supporting a good night's rest. They are mixed with carrier oils (like fractionated coconut oil) and applied to the soles of the feet or are diffused into the air.

Make sure to do your own research before using any essential oils, especially on or around children.

# 47. White Noise

You can get white noise from a fan or from an actual white noise machine. It produces a static sound that the brain subconsciously focuses on, relaxing the mind and body. If you have a toddler that goes to bed great, but has trouble sleeping through the night, trying white noise might be a great option.

# 48. Bore Them To Sleep

Your toddler doesn't want to stay in bed because they are worried they are going to miss out on some exciting party or event you have going on. Well, it's time to burst their little bubble.

This isn't something to do every night, but do give it a try to see if it helps keep them in their bed. Bore them to tears—or at least to sleep!

Don't have the television on. Don't converse with anyone. Just be quiet. You can flip through a magazine or knit—nothing exciting. They will soon find out just how 'fun' it is staying up with mom and dad, and they will actually want to return to their bed.

# 49. Guardian of the Bedroom Galaxy

They are still not staying in bed! Help! Don't give up! You can try putting them to bed, shutting off all the lights, and then sitting on the floor next to the door. Don't talk to them unless they attempt to get out of bed then you may say something like, "Excuse me, please get back in that bed." If they whine or throw requests at you, ignore them. Let them continue to whine.

Play Candy Crush (phone on silent) on your phone, or do something quiet that's not distracting or noticeable to the child. They will realize that there is no getting out of bed, especially with you guarding the door. They will then soon arrive at the much-anticipated destination of Snoozetown.

# 50. Love Always and Forever

Let them know they are the most important thing to you. A child might act out or misbehave at bedtime because they think you are 'off duty' and 'done with them.' You kiss them goodnight, shut the door, and then retreat downstairs without them! They might even hear you laughing or chatting which can make them feel excluded and unloved.

Put yourself in your child's shoes (or in this case, bed). What kind of emotions would you feel in their place? How would you like your mother or father to help you feel better? Truly think about the answers to these questions. See if your perspective has changed a little bit and you feel more empathetic or understanding.

# Conclusion

You succeeded in bringing a new life into this world and survived the first year or so of parenthood. Now you are here in Toddler Land and you may not be enjoying it as much as you think you should, but that will all change. You can learn to love being in Toddler Land.

There's a lot to enjoy about having a toddler. They are full of curiosity and they are so excited about testing out their new-found sense of independence! They start tippy-toeing to their boundaries and seeing how far they can stretch them. They find the world a strange, funny, but wonderful place. Everything is new and exciting to them.

A trip to the grocery store is thrilling! A walk around the block contains excitement at every step—so many leaves and pieces of dirt to pick up! Visiting the grandparents and being cooed over and fed chocolate chip cookies and chocolate milk just because they are the 'sweetest, most angelic, wonderful, beautiful child that ever lived.' Wouldn't it be great to live each day with this much enthusiasm and excitement?

Your toddler gets to wake up each morning with so much excitement and joy. Sometimes they don't act the way we expect them to, and we need to understand that it's perfectly okay. They are learning about their new world. Their brains are excitedly creating neuro-connections and tracks all over the place—trying to put together all the new things they are learning.

There is no such thing as a perfect child. There is also no such thing as a perfect adult. Keep your expectations for your child in check. Make sure your expectations aren't way above the capabilities and skillset of your child. Just like Dr. Ross Greene said, "Children do well if they can." There is no child on this earth that wants to misbehave and cause problems.

It is up to you to guide and teach your child how to behave. Instill in them at a young age to treat others the way they like to be treated, (i.e. "the golden rule"). Yelling at your child or resorting to spanking is teaching your child that type of behavior is acceptable and okay. This in turn can cause your child to yell and act aggressively towards others. In several years you definitely don't want to get a phone call from your child's school saying that your son or daughter beat up another kid for accidentally bumping into them in the hallway.

Now you may say, 'Well, spanking is the only thing that works for my child because they are so strong-willed and don't respond to anything else. Spanking is the only thing that makes them stop misbehaving and listen to me.' Unfortunately, you are not alone in feeling this way. Did you know that according to a 2014 UNICEF report, more than 80% of children worldwide are spanked?

So, yes, you are definitely not alone in thinking that spanking is working, but a recent study done by two professors at the University of Michigan and the University of Texas-Austin, found that spanking actually doesn't give you immediate results or have positive long-term effects. The study defines spanking as 'swatting on the behind with an open hand.'

After analyzing over fifty years of data collected, it was determined that there is in fact a direct correlation between children that were spanked and kids that display delinquent and aggressive behavior. It was also found that older kids and teenagers that suffer from depression and anxiety were most often found to have been spanked as a child.

Again, the 'golden rule.' By teaching your child to spank, you are neglecting to teach them important conflict resolution skills. By following the fifty tips and ideas that cover everything from how to handle or discipline your child in a public setting, to how to handle the daily bedtime misadventures—you'll set yourself and your child up for success!

Comedian Jerry Seinfeld says, *"A two-year old is kind of like having a blender, but you don't have the top for it. "*

Well guess what? You now have a top for that blender!

# Final Words

Congratulations on finishing this book. I hope you enjoyed this book and know now how to discipline your toddler.

**If you liked the book, would you do me a huge favor and write a review on Amazon?**

Your review is really important and it will help other parents know what to expect from the book.

It will really encourage me to write more books for you.

I look forward to reading your review.

Bye for now, and take care!

Jessica Riley

Jessica Riley

www.ingramcontent.com/pod-product-compliance
Lightning Source LLC
LaVergne TN
LVHW021541080426
835509LV00019B/2770